THIS NOTEBOOK BELONGS TO ....

CONTACT ....

See our range of fine, illustrated books, ebooks, notebooks and art calendars:
www.flametreepublishing.com

This is a **FLAME TREE NOTEBOOK**
Published and © copyright 2017 Flame Tree Publishing Ltd

FTNB 154 • 978-1-78664-619-4

Cover image based on a detail from
Sophia and the Unicorn
©ElXi-Ameyn

The woman's white dress aligns her with the white unicorn, an allusion to her virtue and innocence. Brilliantly coloured leaves speckle the enchanting blue background of the hidden lake the two are crossing. The light appears to be radiating from the unicorn's golden, magic horn which casts a glow onto the woman's face like a halo.

FLAME TREE PUBLISHING I The Art of Fine Gifts
6 Melbray Mews, London SW6 3NS, United Kingdom